LAND OF SPIRITS

AN **UNOFFICIAL** COLORING BOOK

LAND OF SPIRITS

Published by:
Ulysses Press
PO Box 3440
Berkeley, CA 94703
www.ulyssespress.com

ISBN: 978-1-64604-588-4

Printed in the United States by Kingery Printing Company
10 9 8 7 6 5 4 3 2 1

IMPORTANT NOTE TO READERS: This book is an independent and unauthorized fan publication. No endorsement, license, sponsorship, or affiliation with Hayao Miyazaki, his publishers, or Studio Ghibli, or other copyright or trademark holders is claimed or suggested. All references in this book to copyrighted or trademarked characters and other elements of Studio Ghibli are the property of their respective owners and used for informational purposes only. All trademarked products that appear in the book are the property of their respective owners and used for informational purposes only. The author and publisher encourage readers to watch, rent, purchase, and support Studio Ghibli, and to patronize the brands pictured in this book.

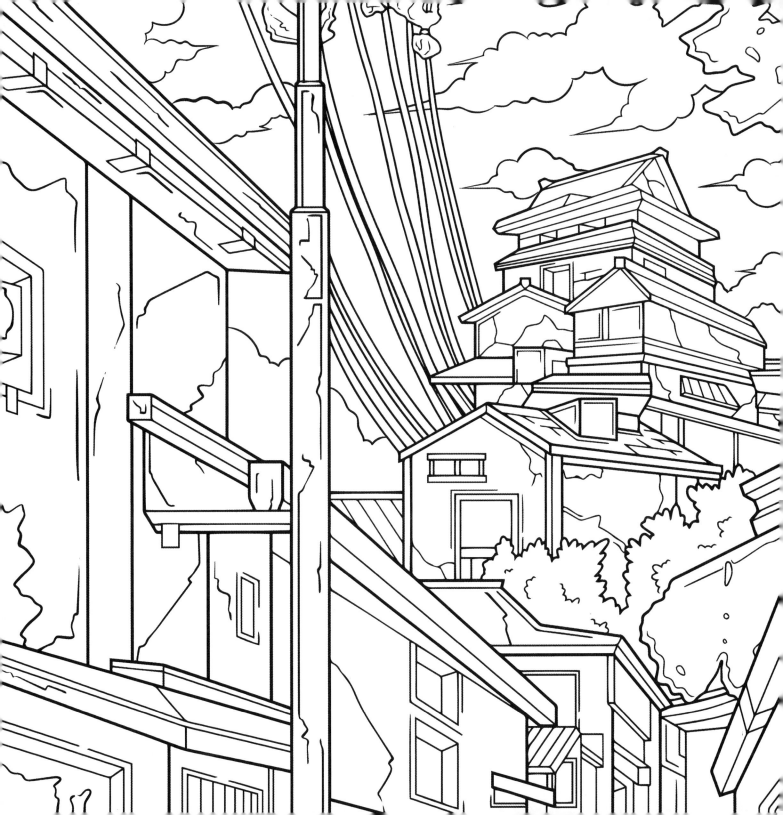

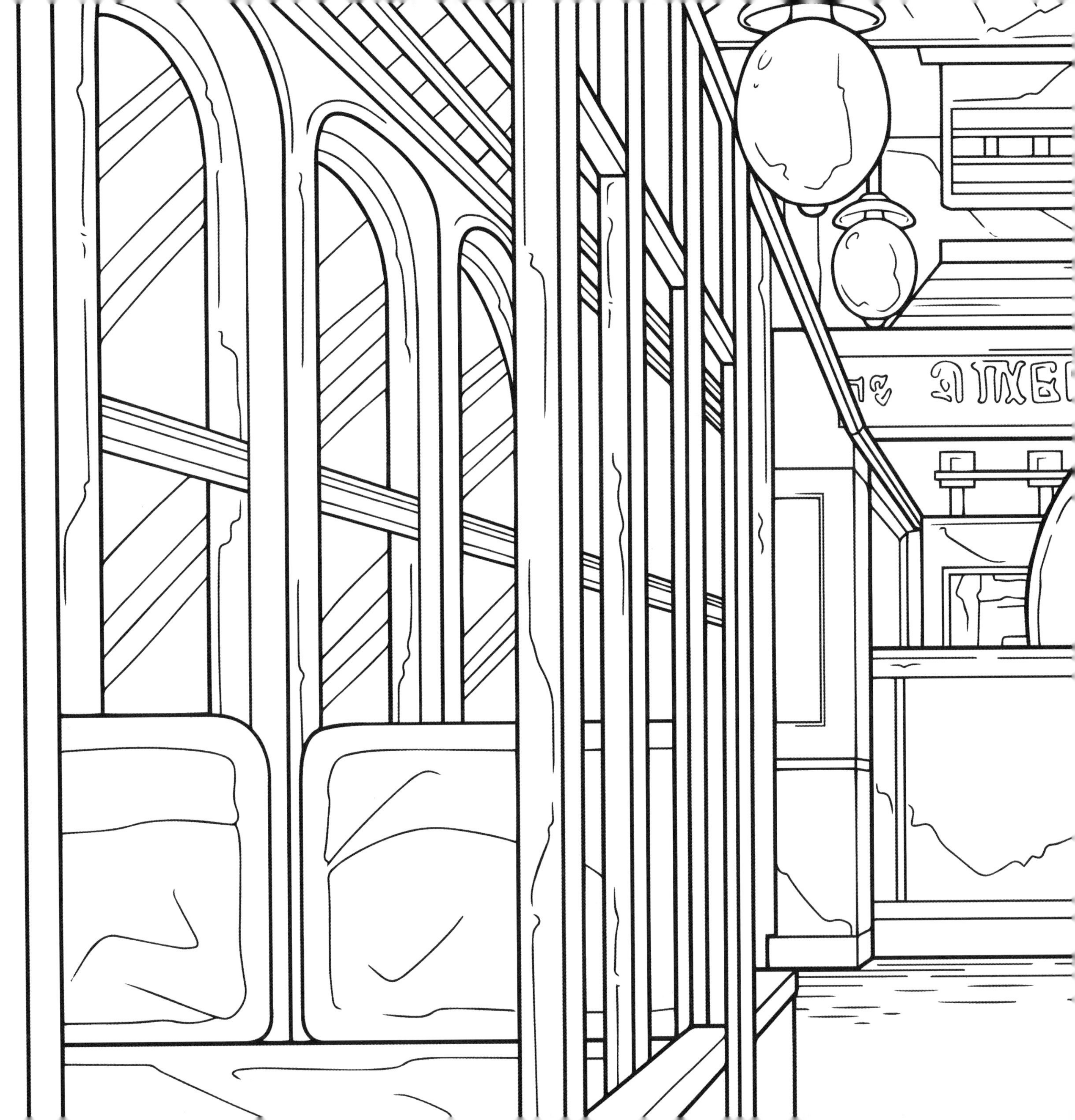

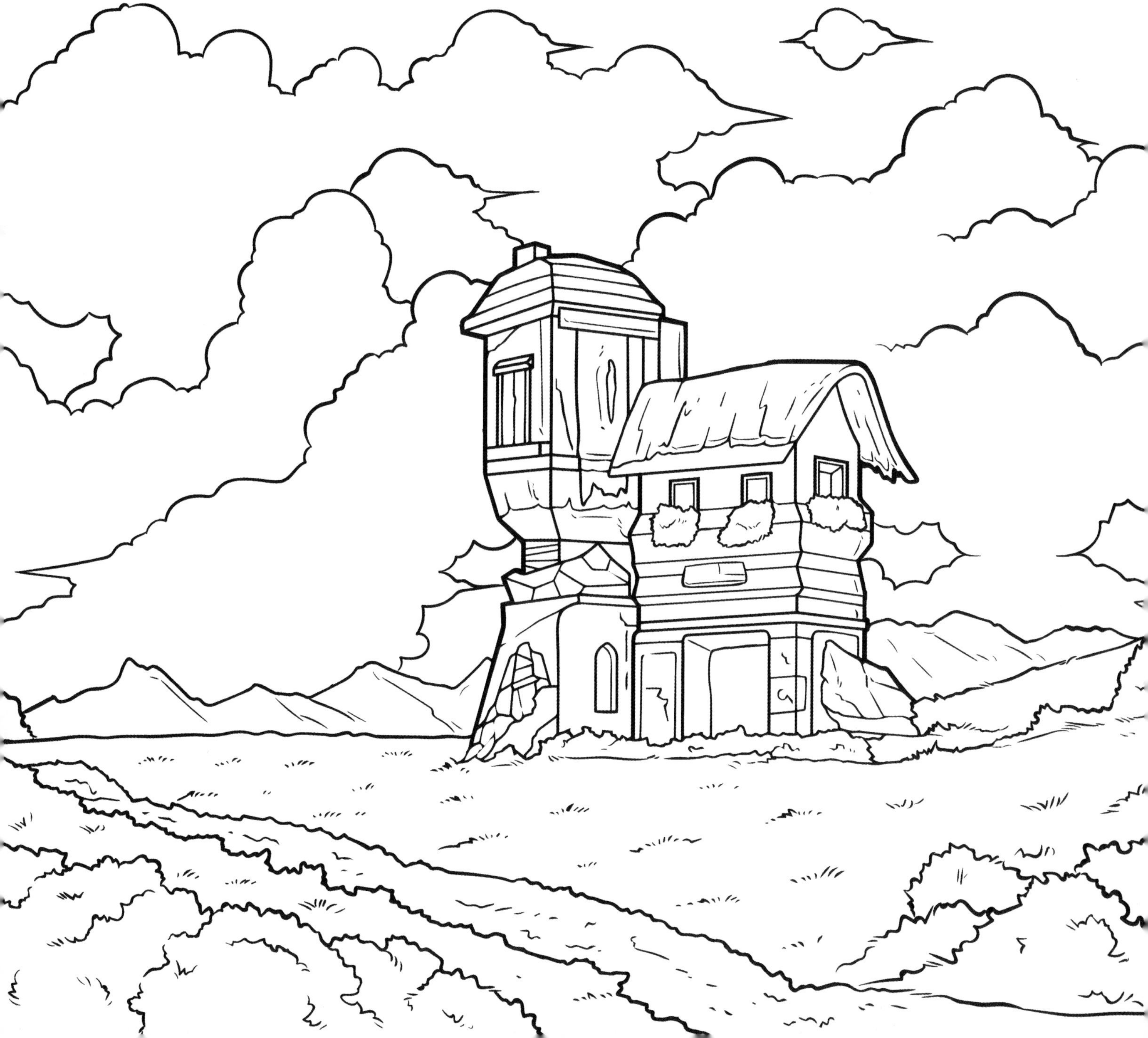

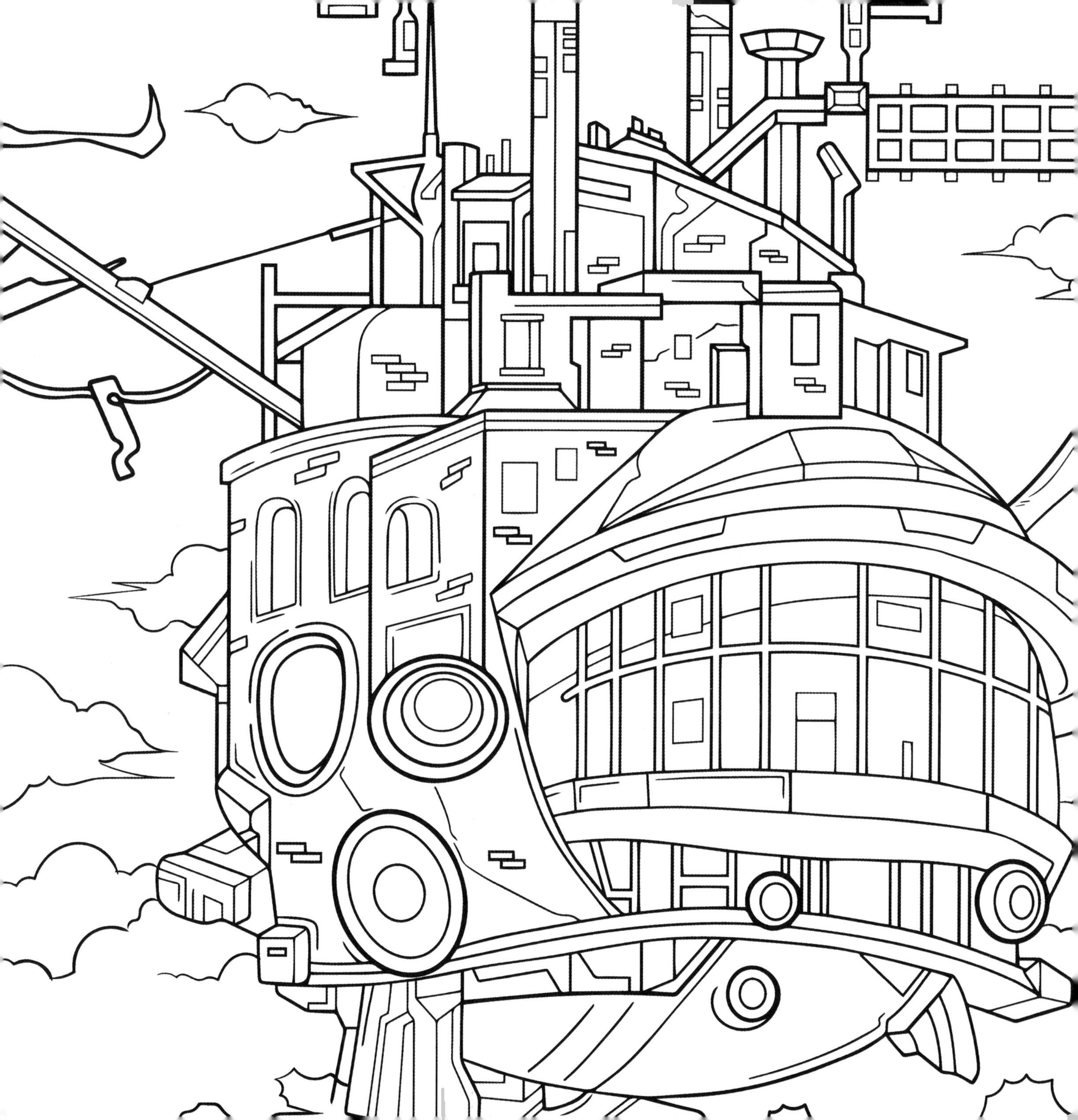

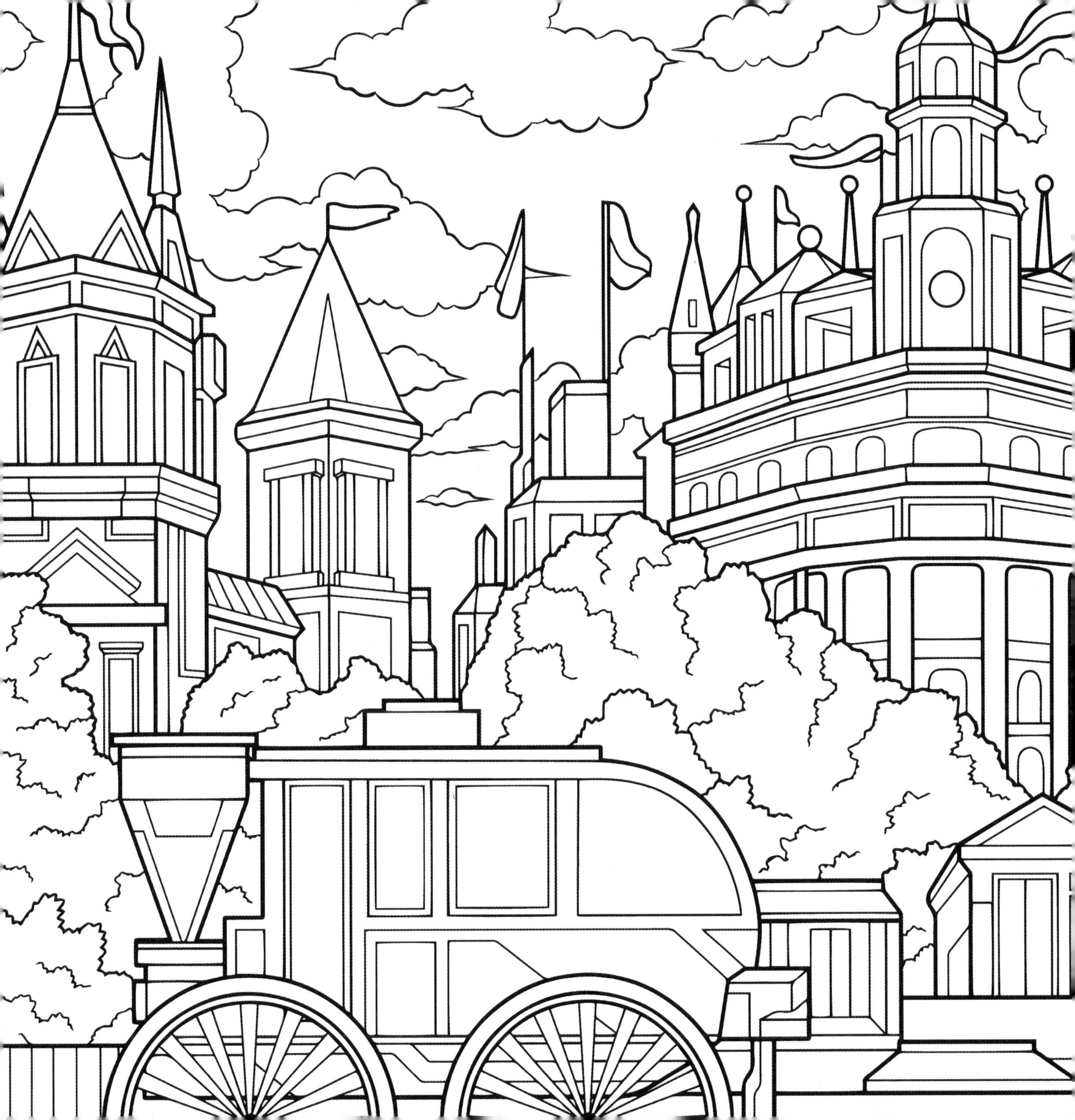

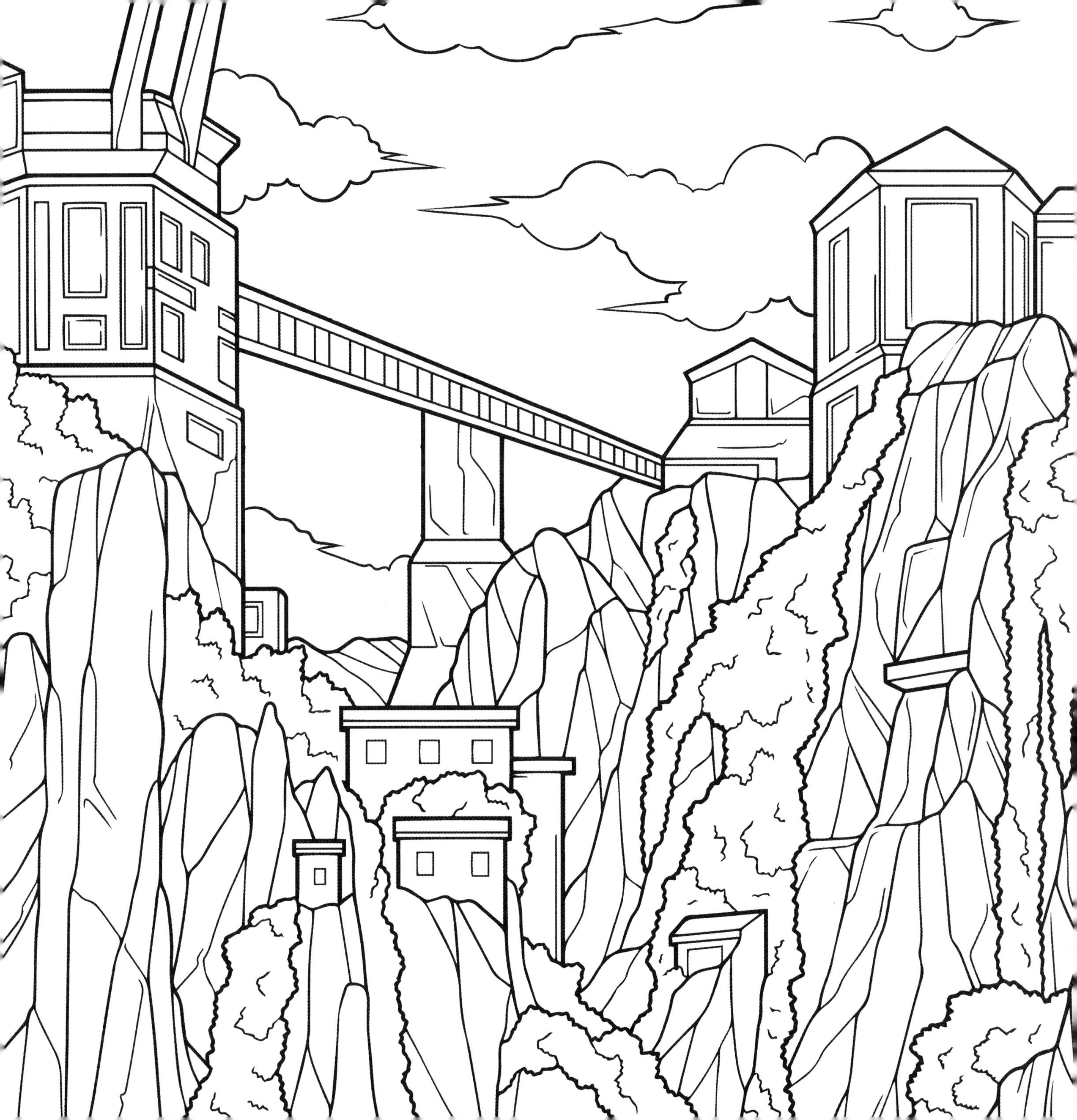

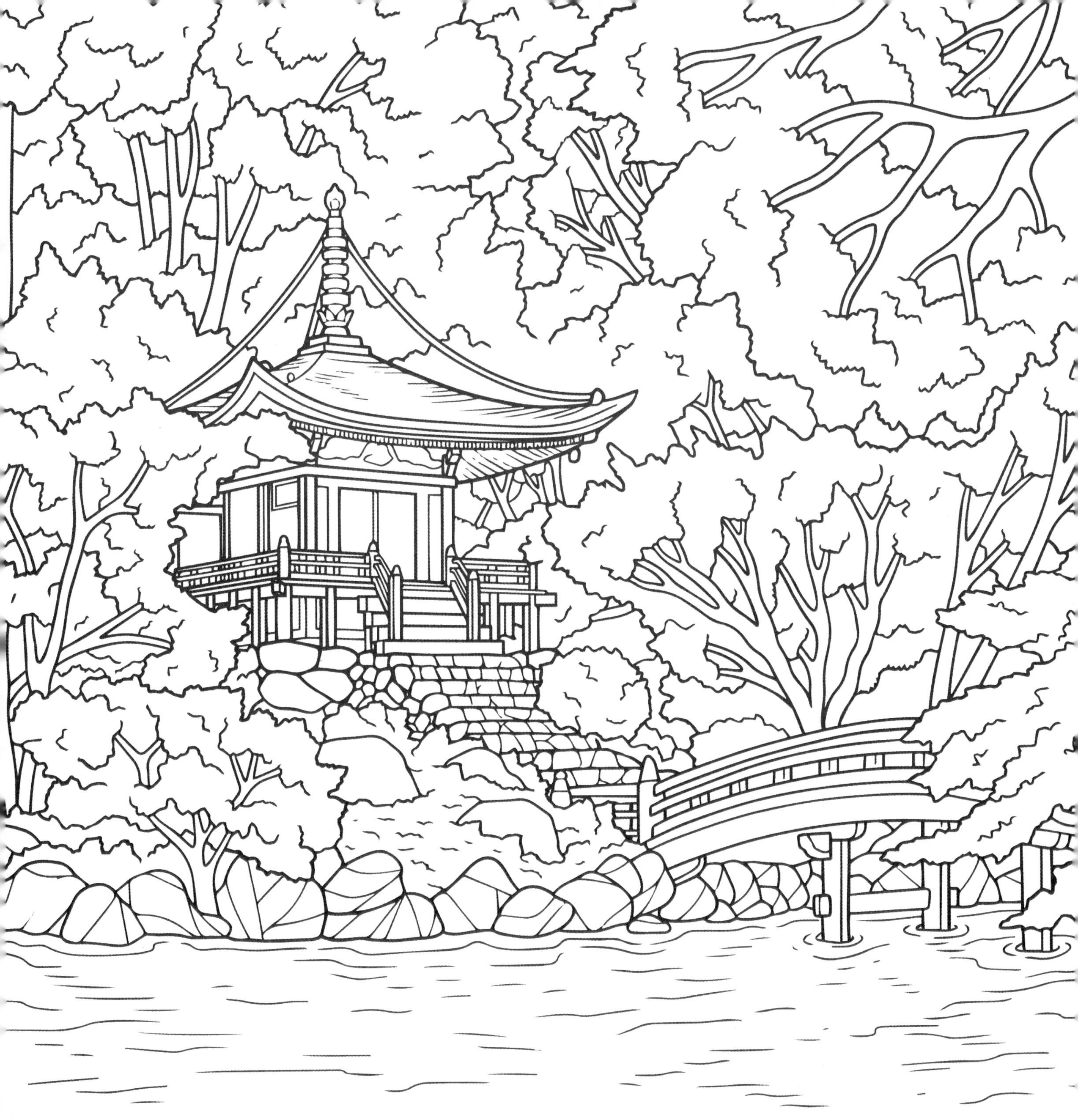

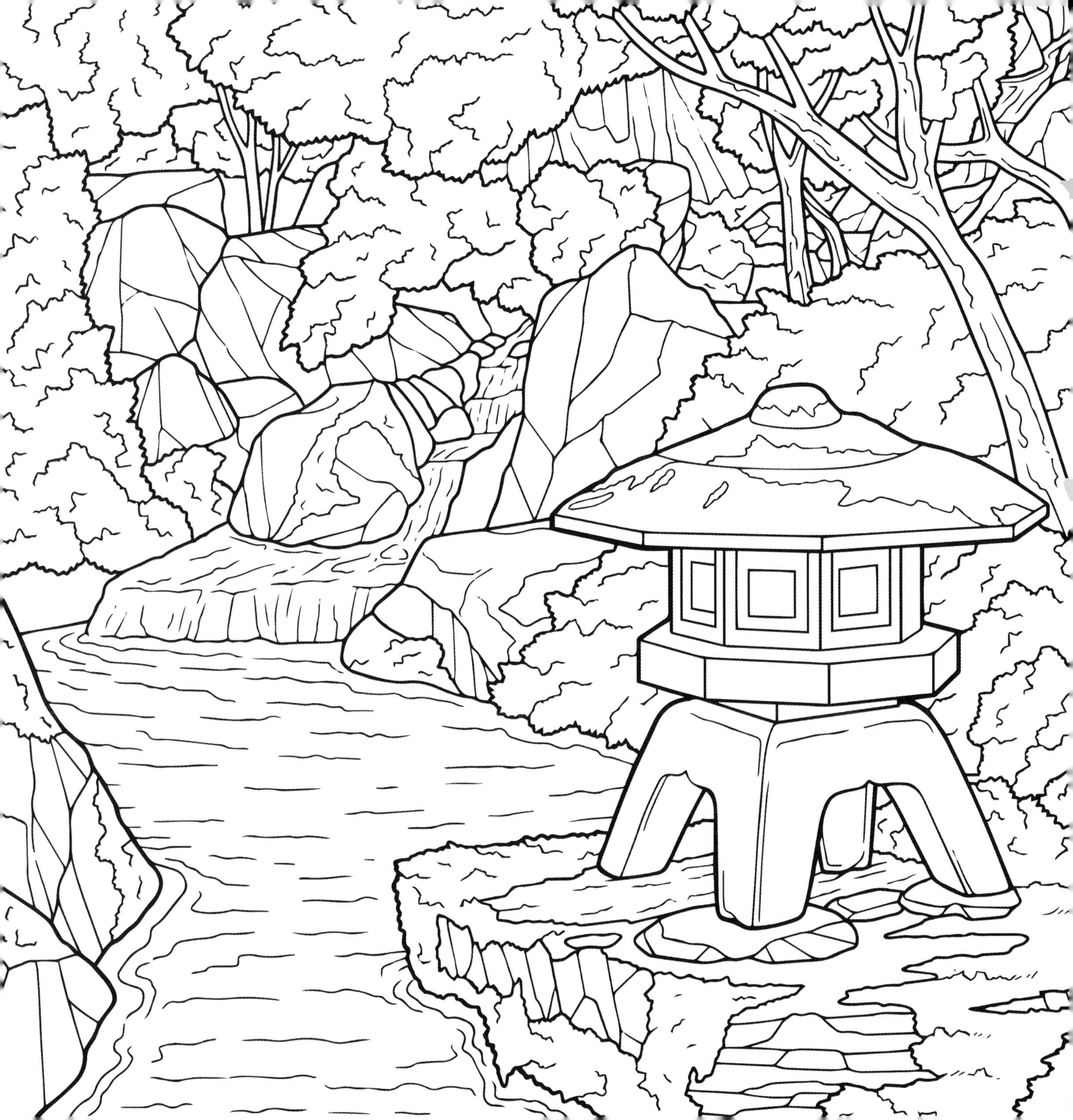

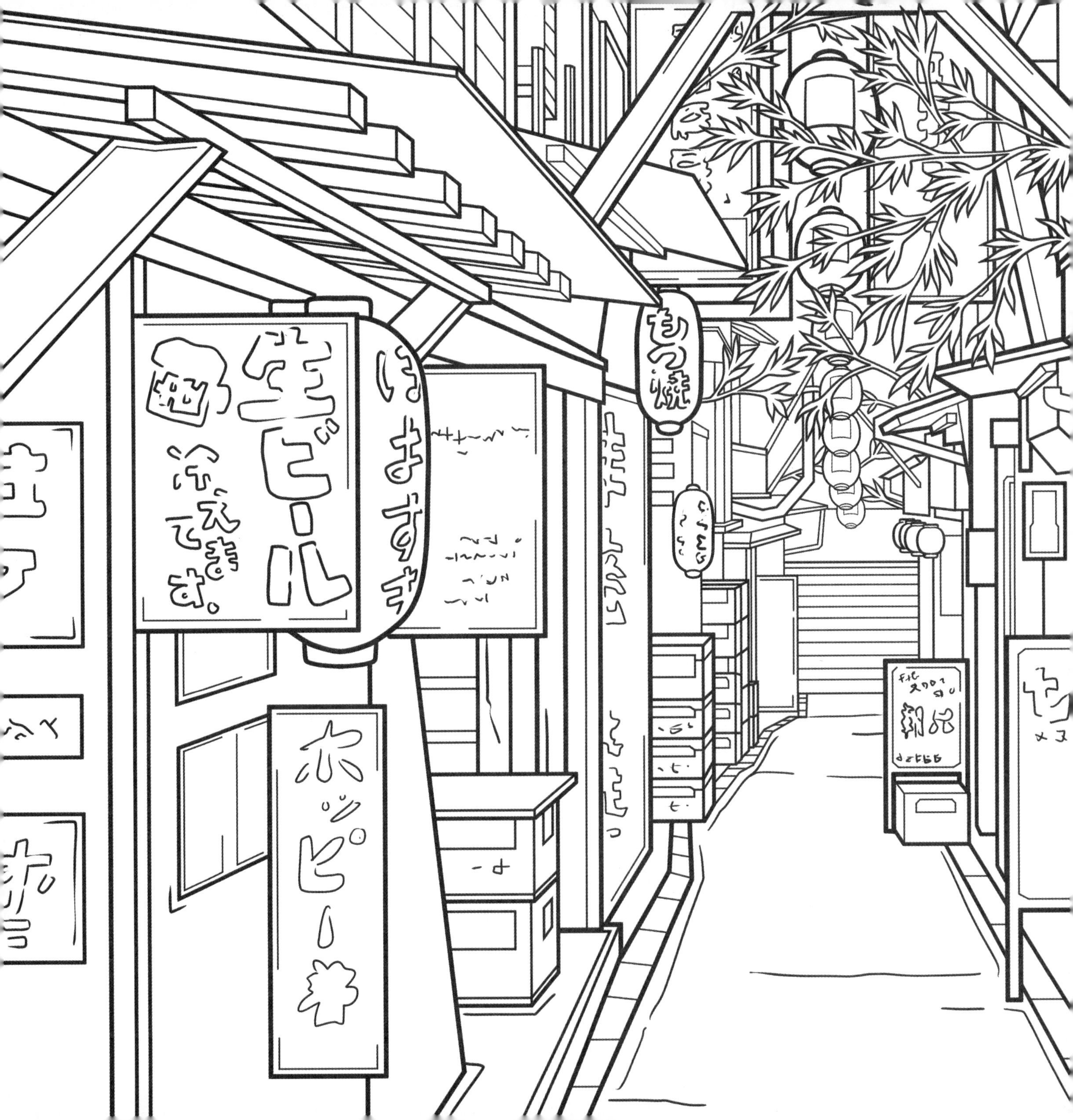
生ビール
冷えてます。
もつ焼
ホッピー

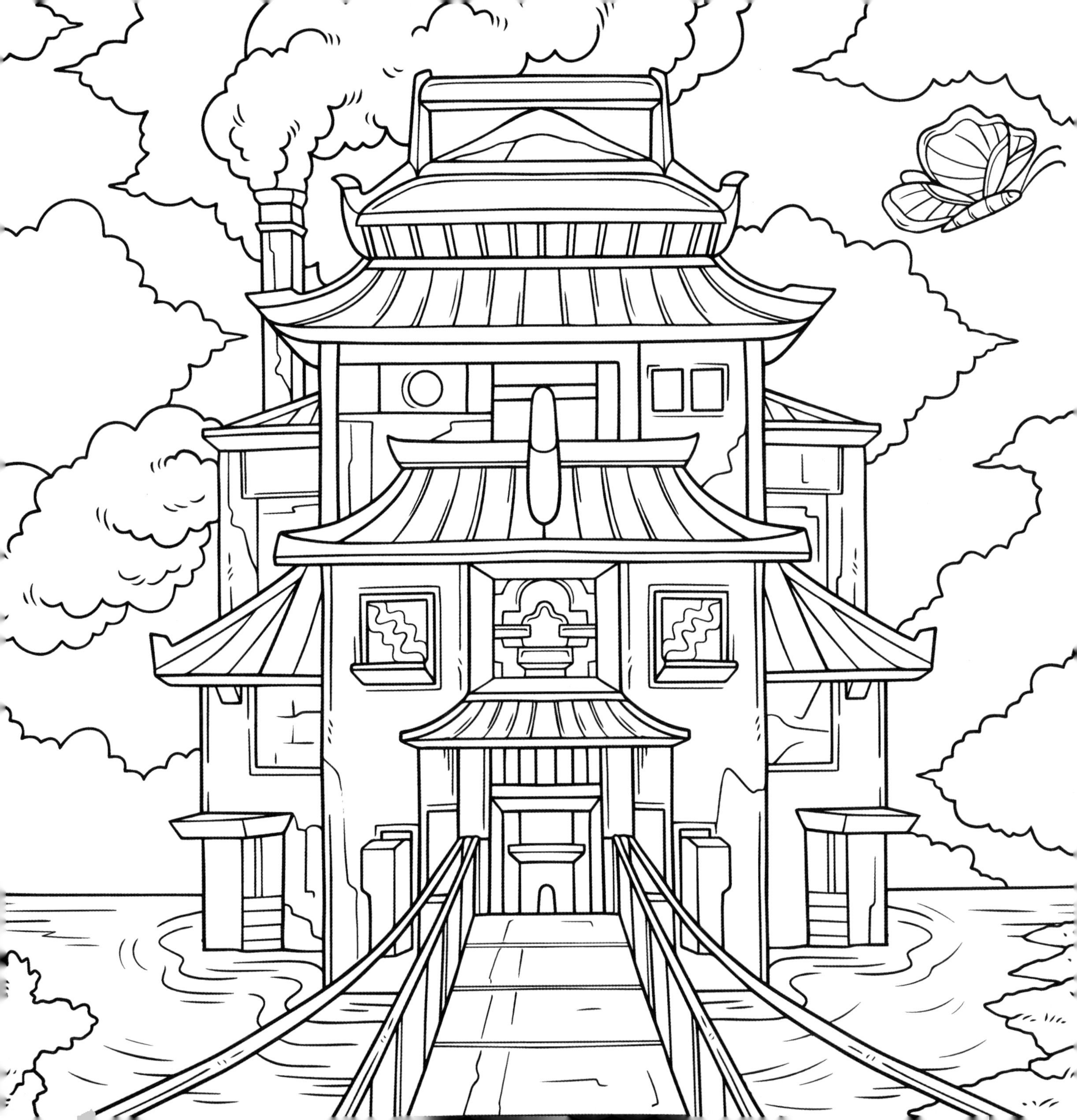

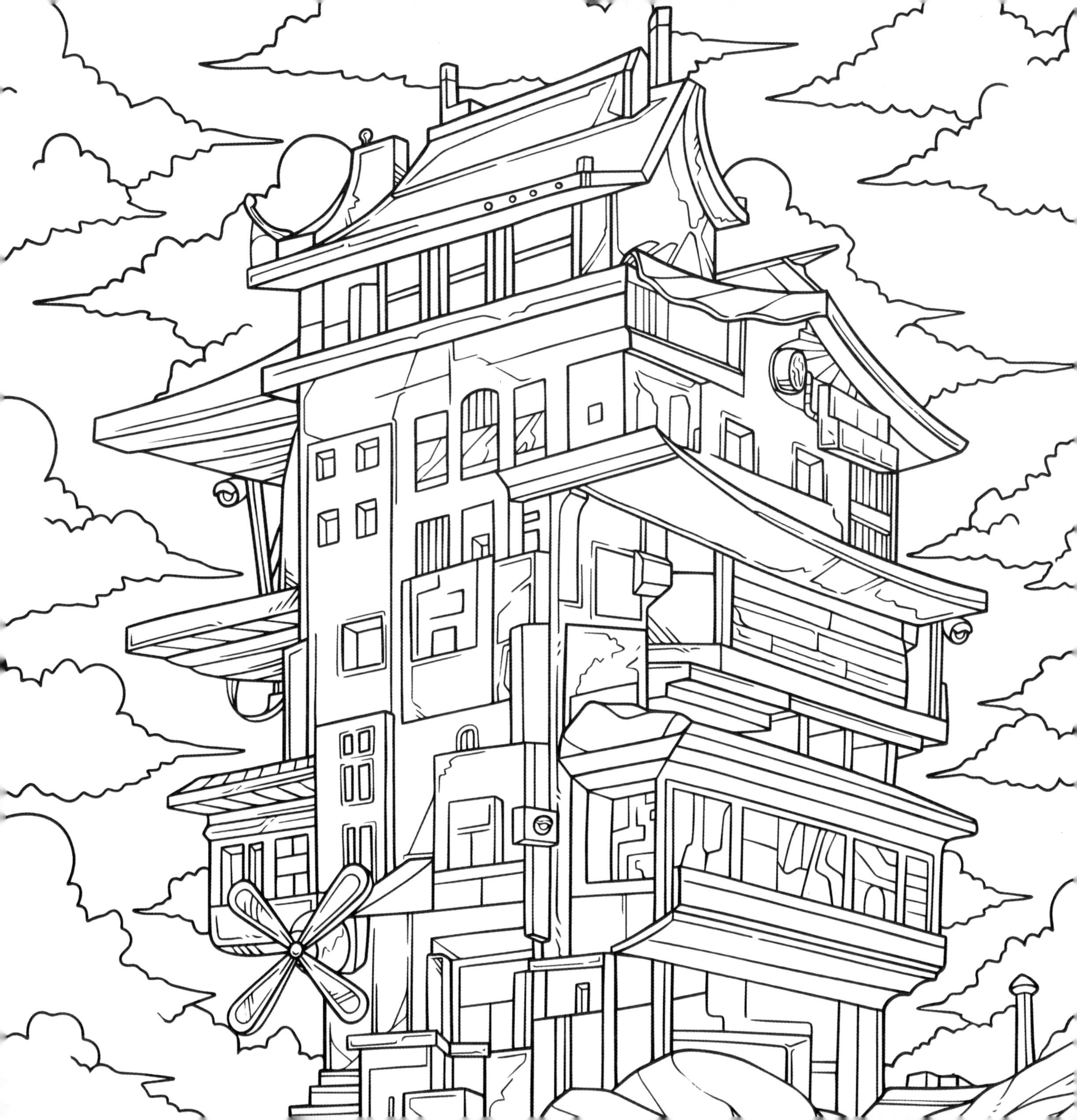

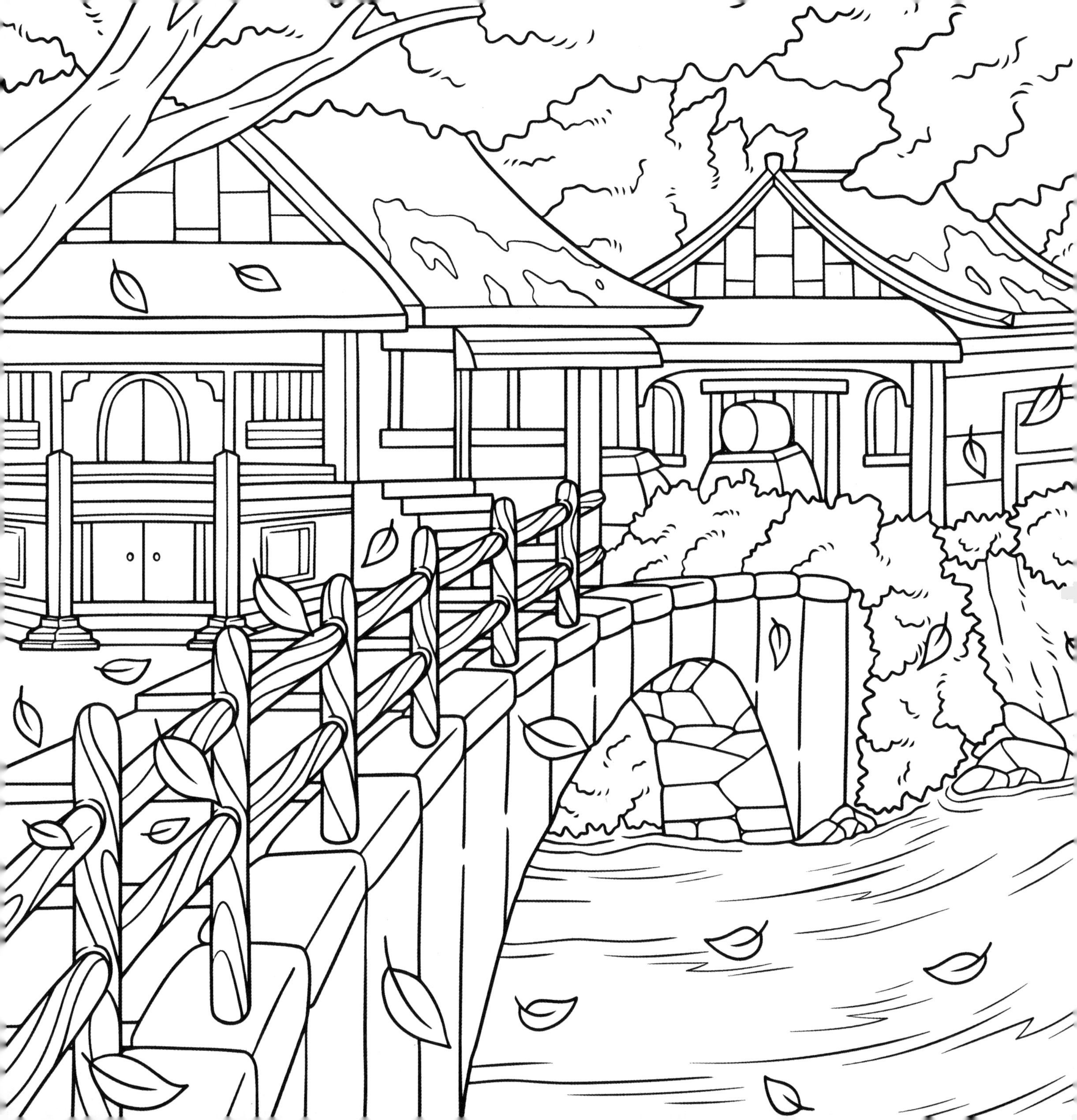

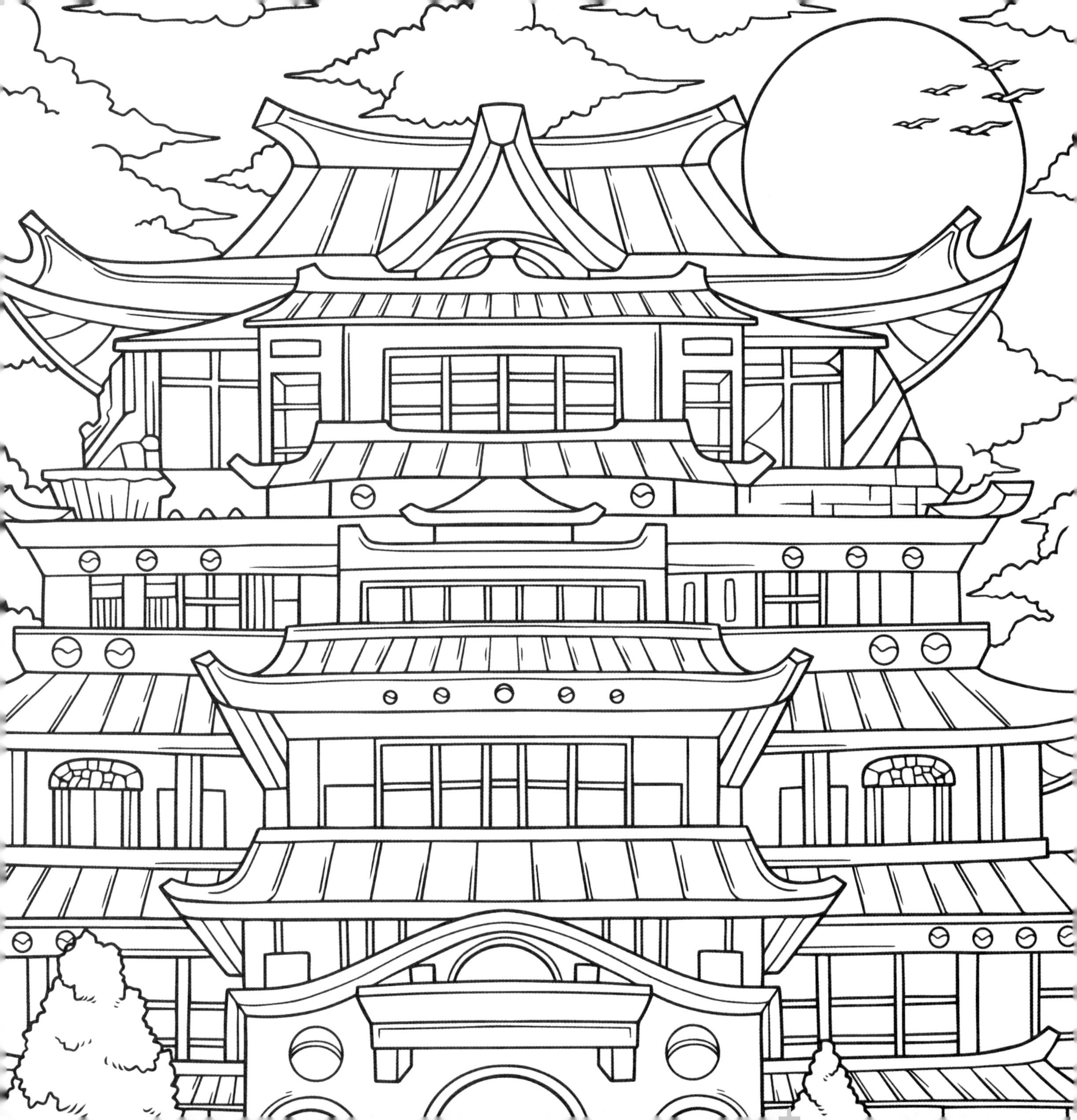

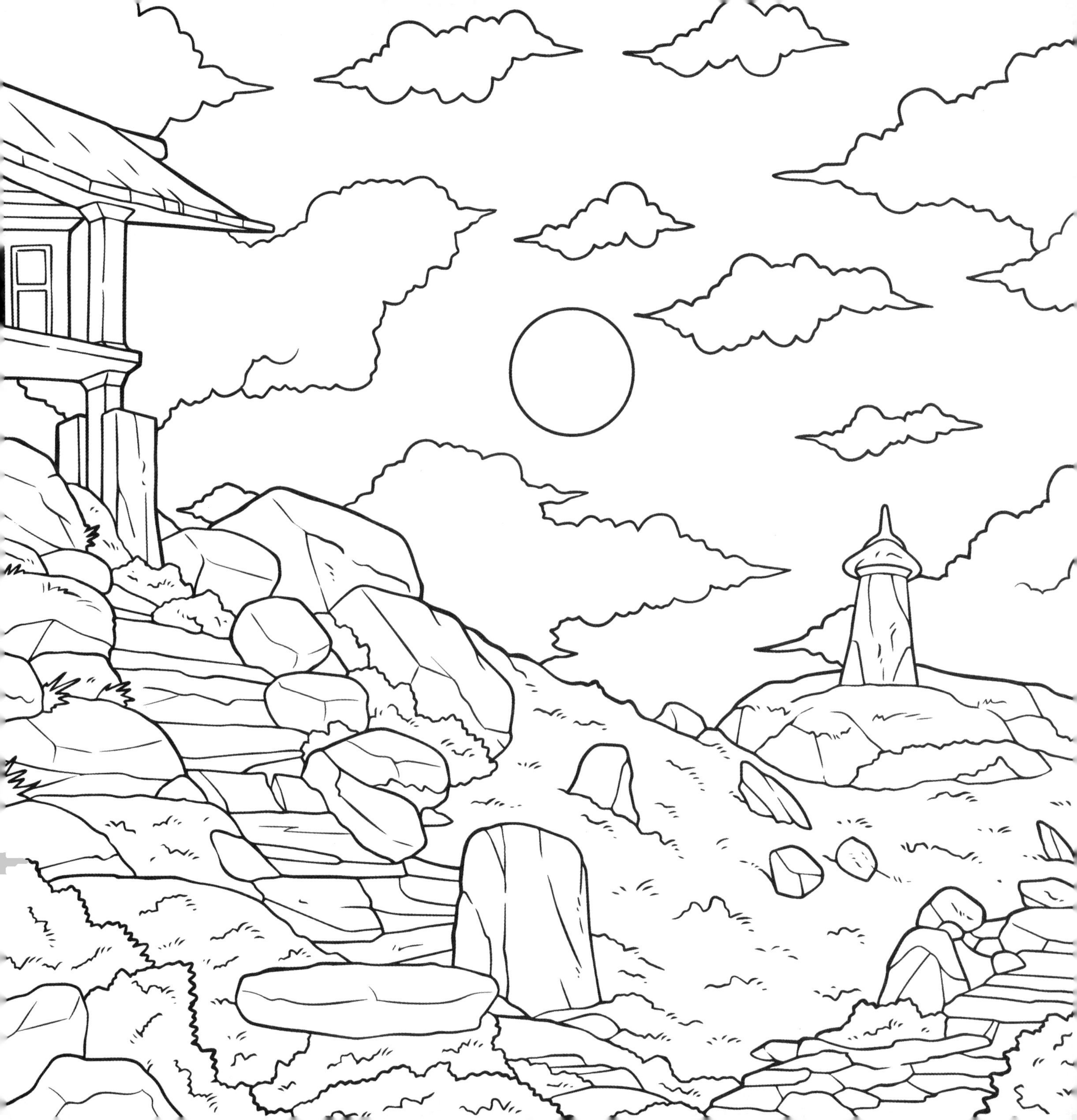

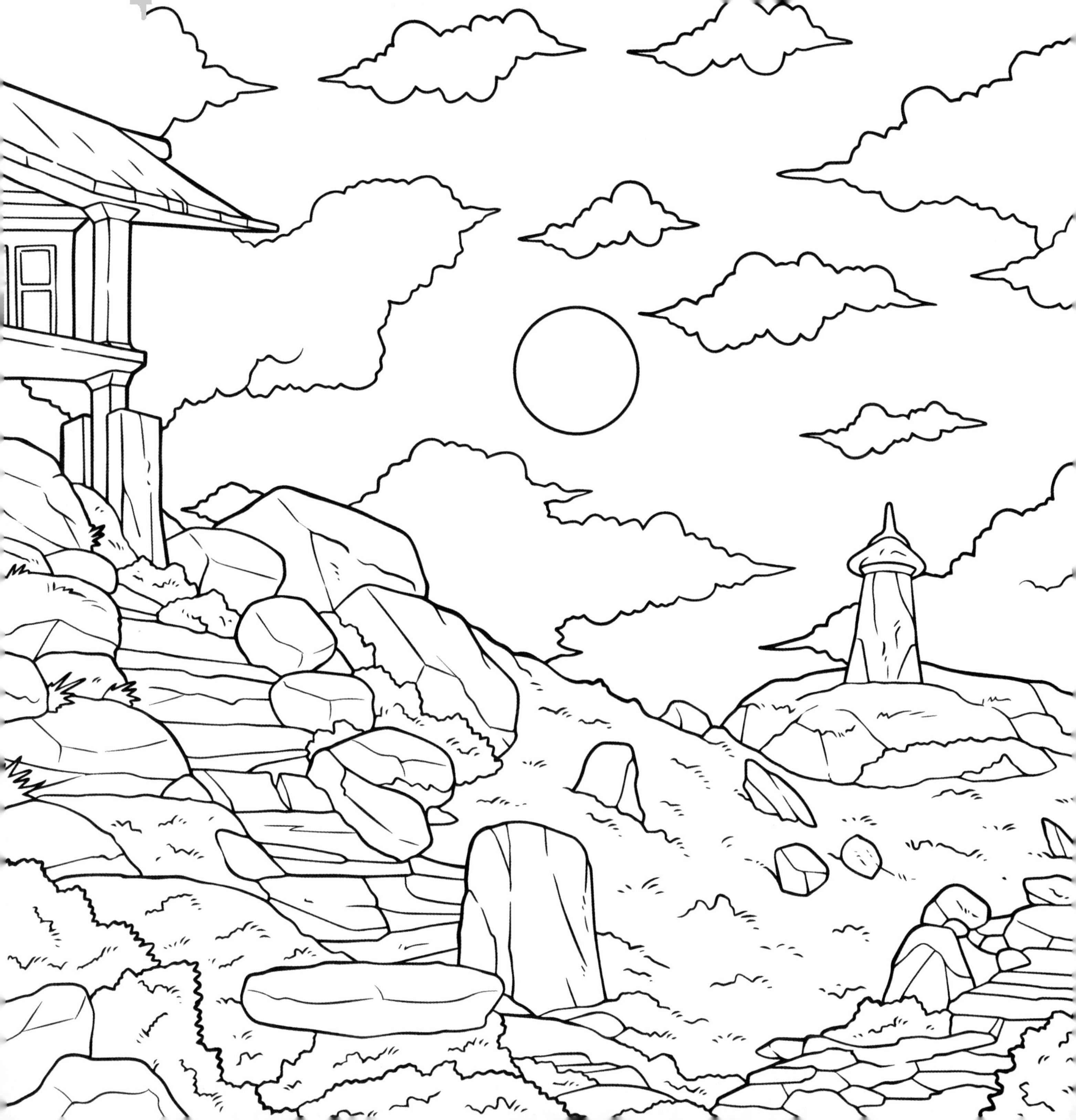

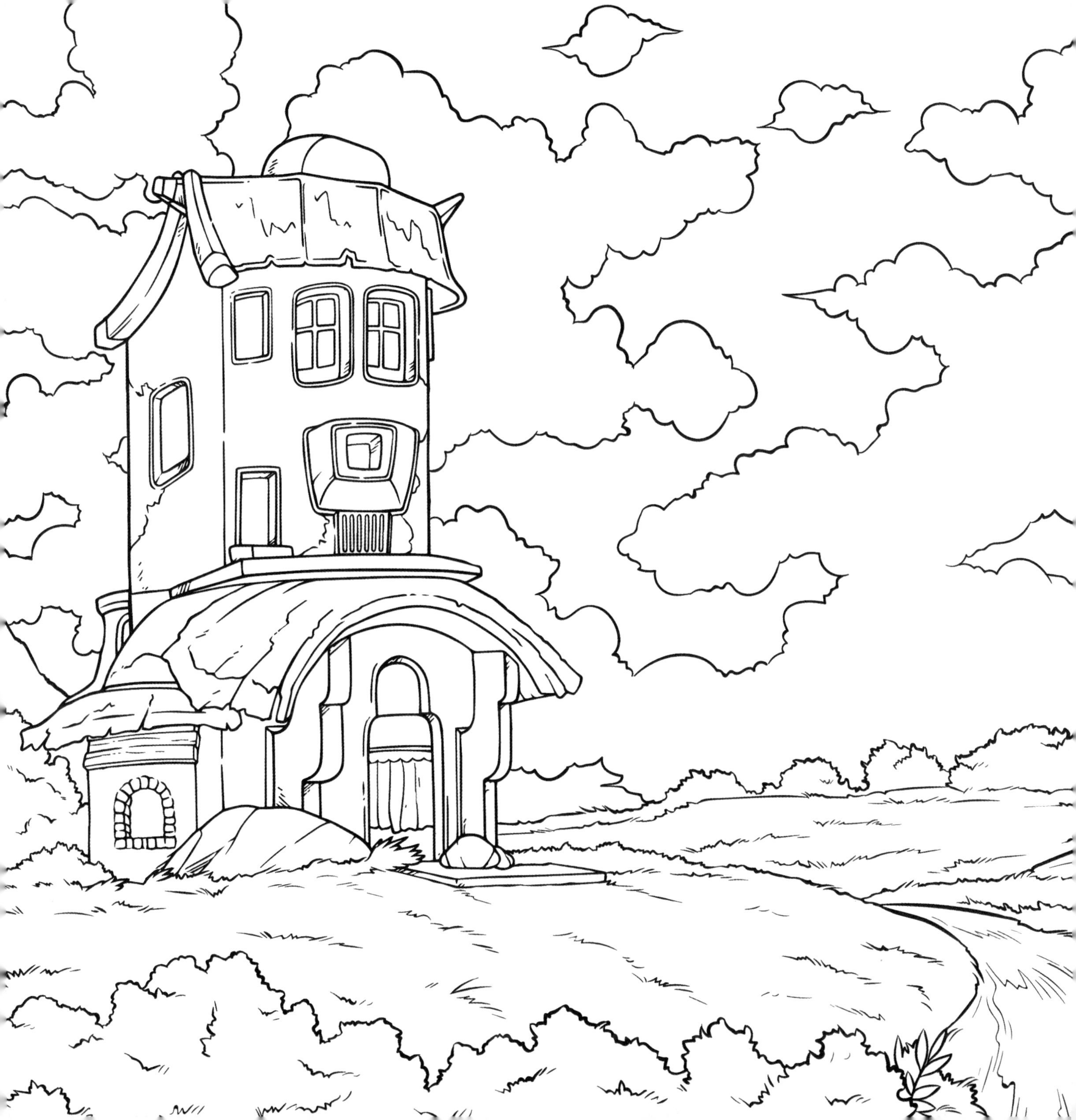

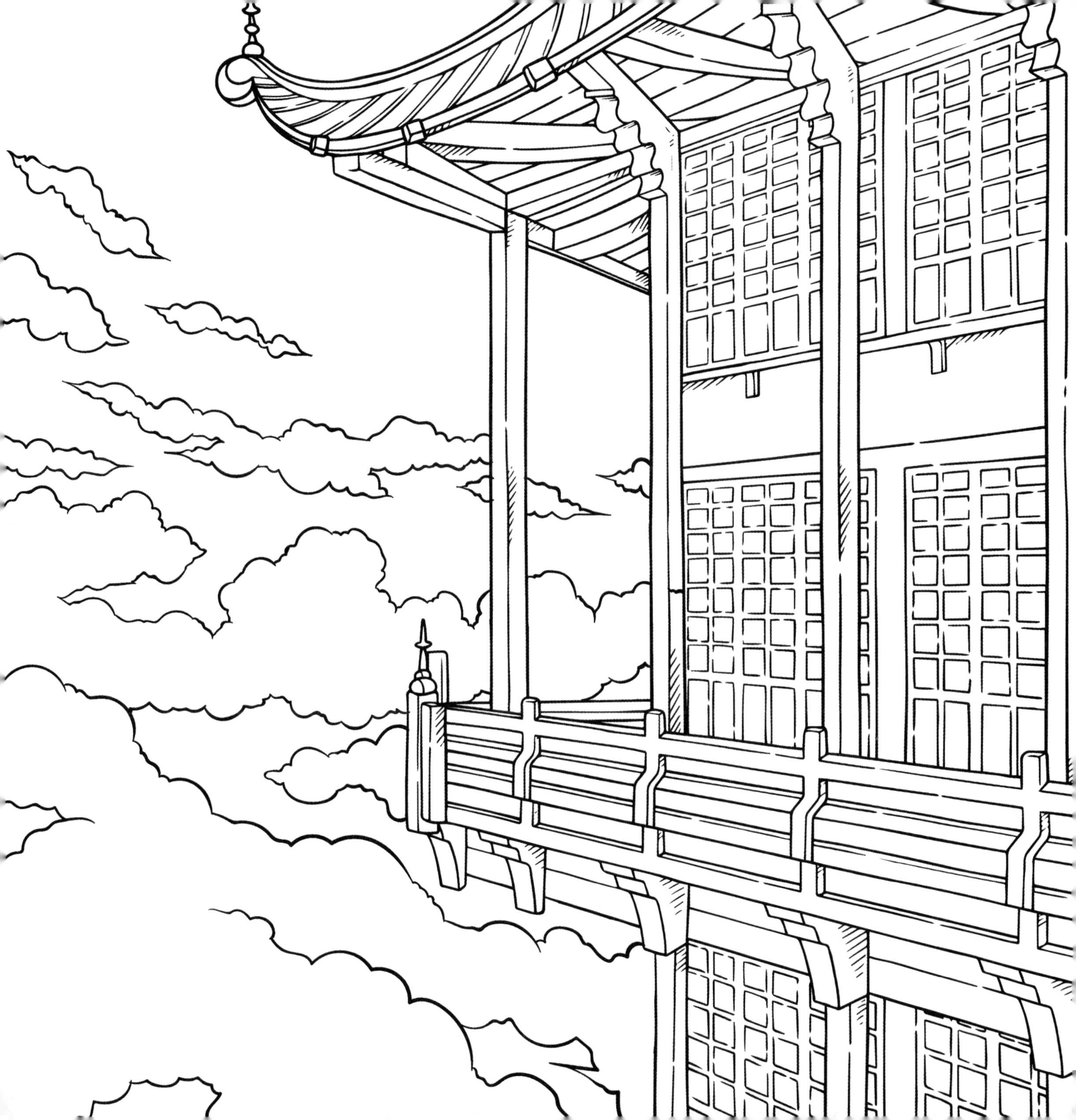

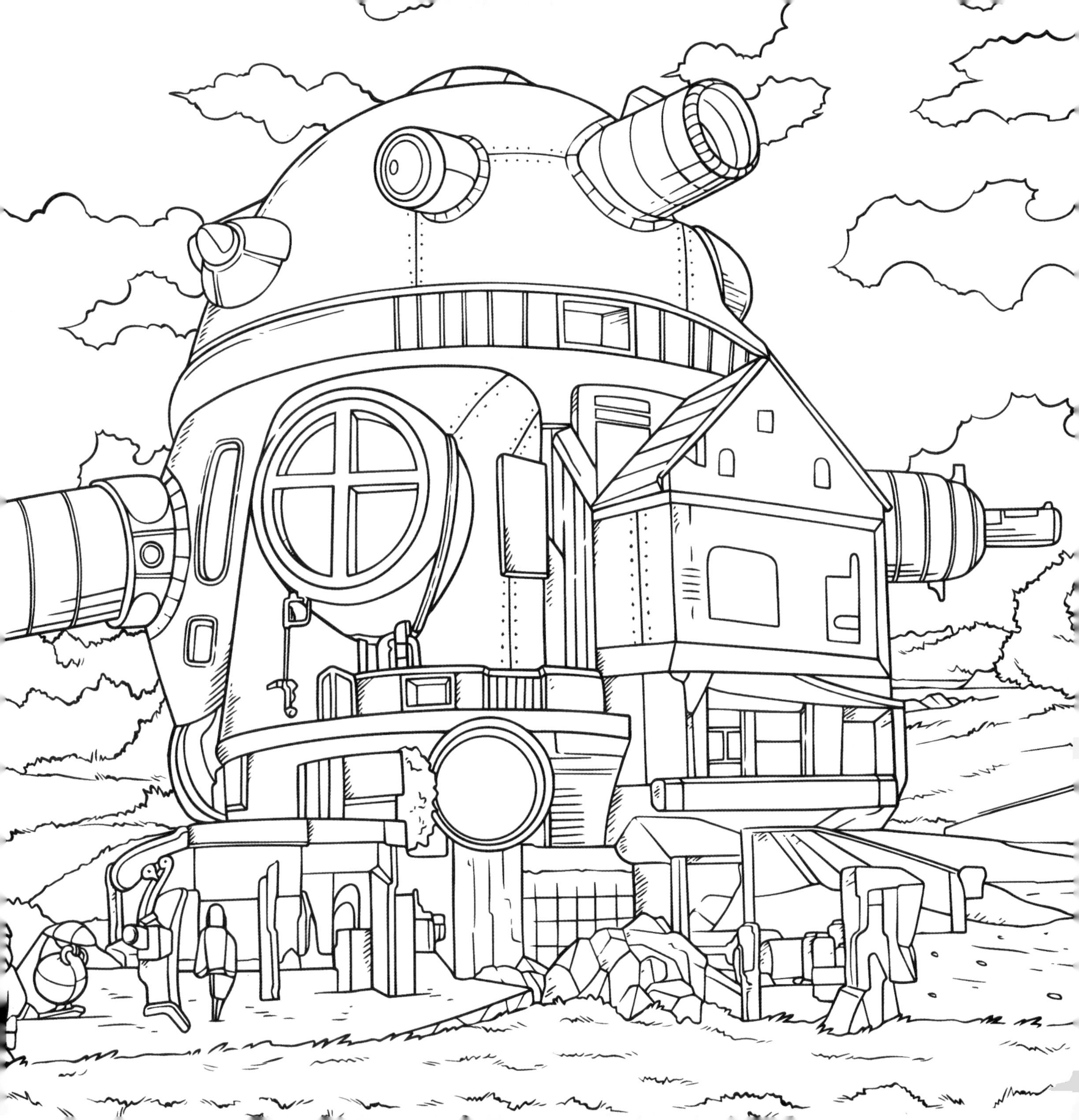

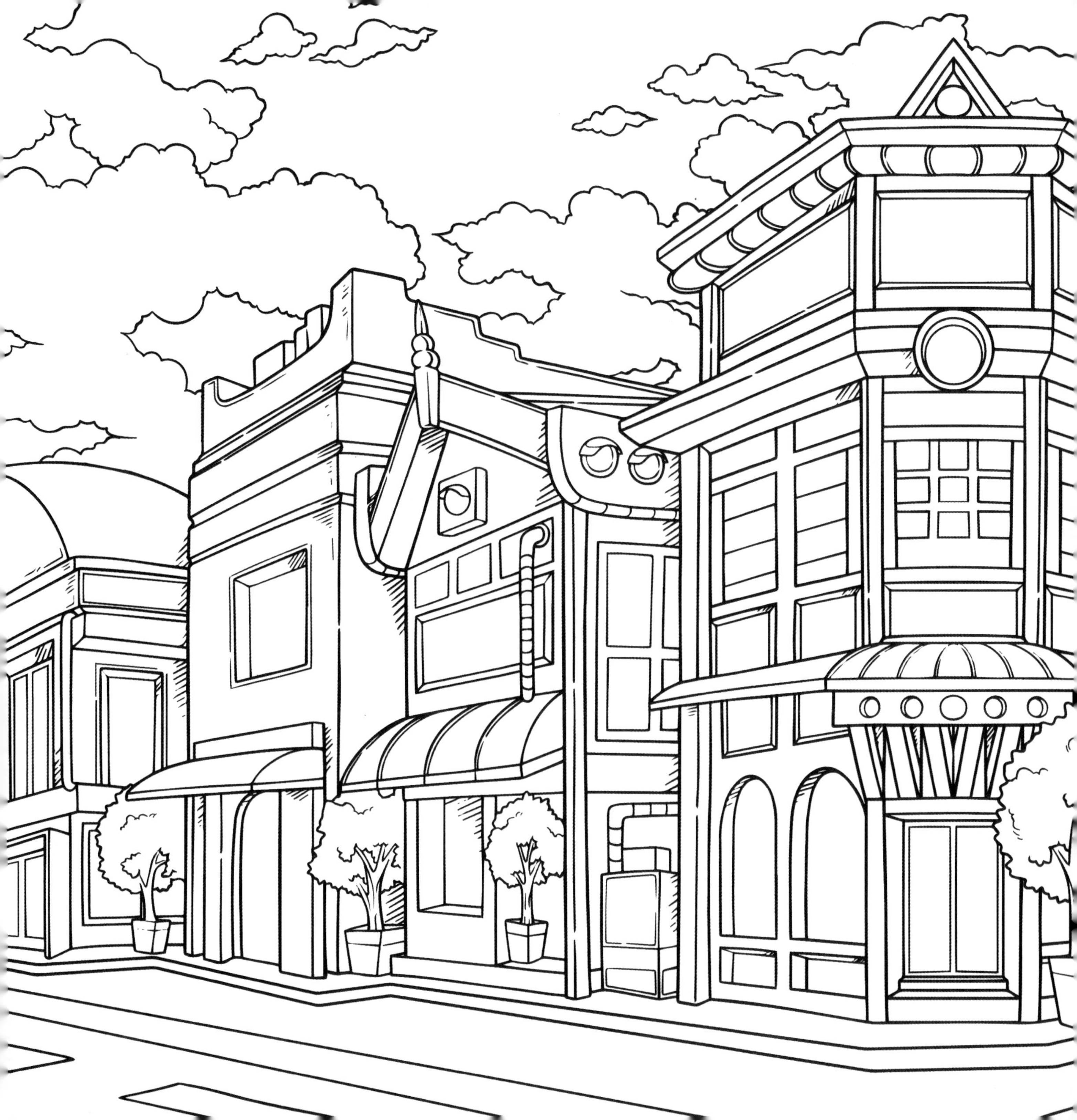

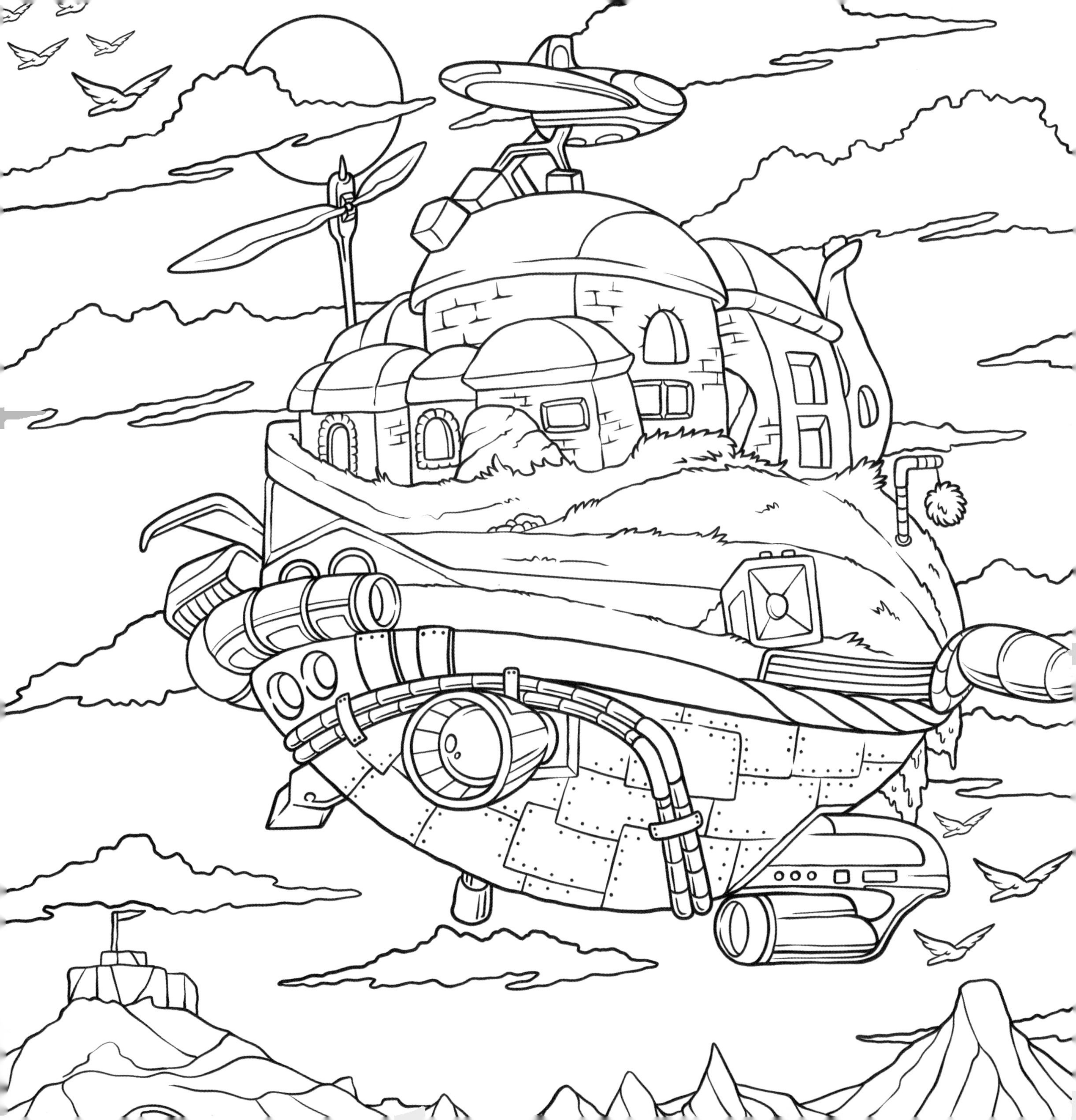

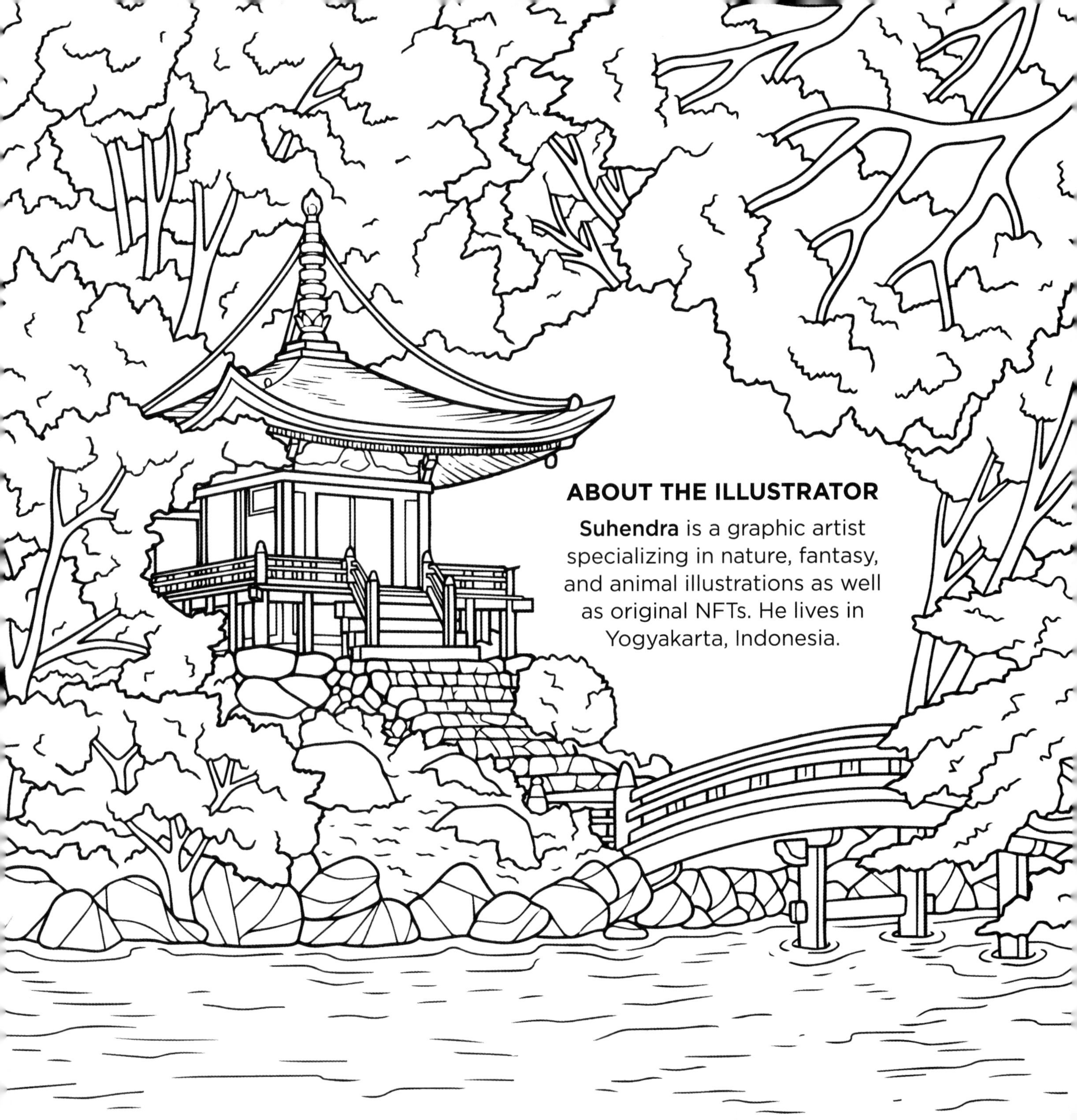

ABOUT THE ILLUSTRATOR

Suhendra is a graphic artist specializing in nature, fantasy, and animal illustrations as well as original NFTs. He lives in Yogyakarta, Indonesia.

Discover More Great Coloring Books from Ulysses Press

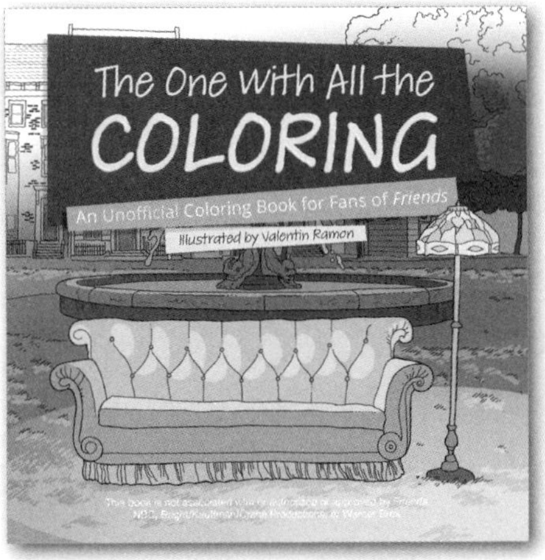
The One With All the
COLORING
An Unofficial Coloring Book for Fans of Friends
Illustrated by Valentin Ramon

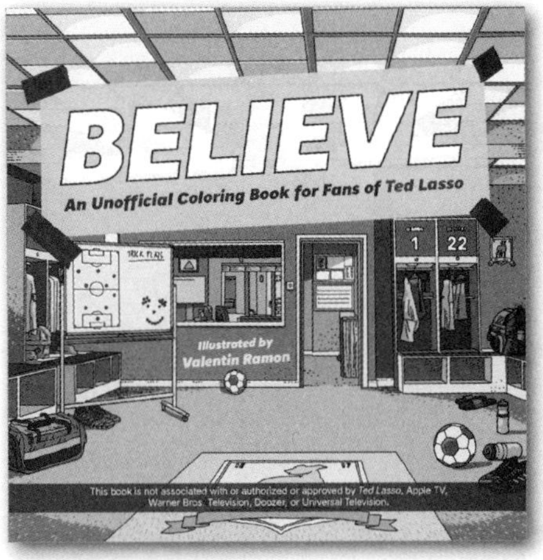
BELIEVE
An Unofficial Coloring Book for Fans of Ted Lasso
Illustrated by
Valentin Ramon
This book is not associated with or authorized or approved by Ted Lasso, Apple TV, Warner Bros. Television, Doozer, or Universal Television.

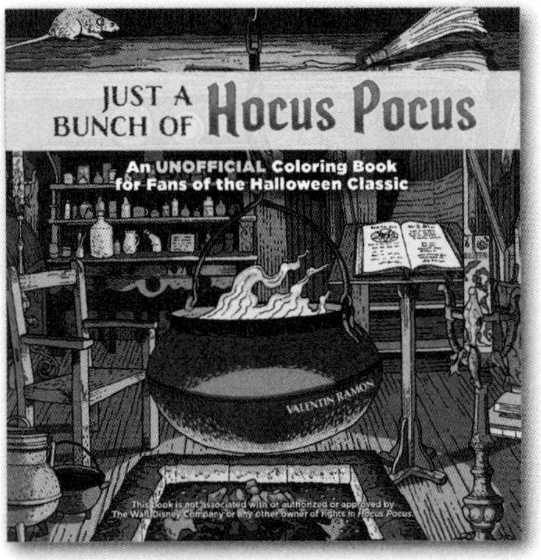
JUST A BUNCH OF Hocus Pocus
An UNOFFICIAL Coloring Book for Fans of the Halloween Classic
VALENTIN RAMON
This book is not associated with or authorized or approved by The Walt Disney Company or any other owner of rights in Hocus Pocus.

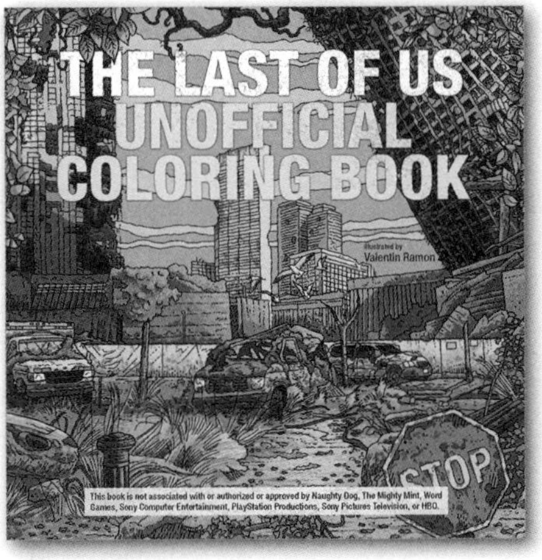
THE LAST OF US
UNOFFICIAL
COLORING BOOK
Illustrated by
Valentin Ramon
STOP
This book is not associated with or authorized or approved by Naughty Dog, The Mighty Mint, Word Games, Sony Computer Entertainment, PlayStation Productions, Sony Pictures Television, or HBO.

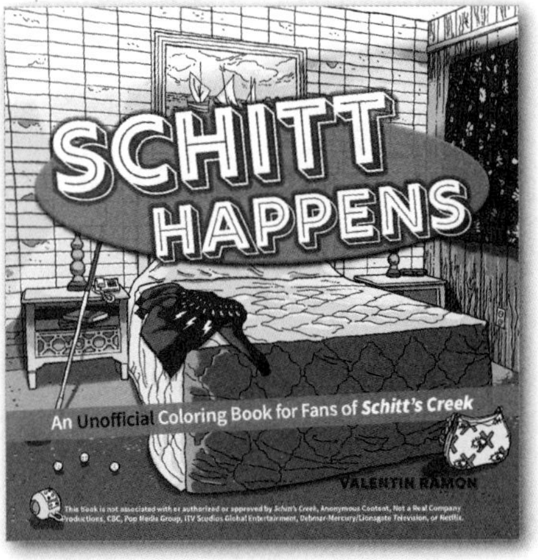
SCHITT
HAPPENS
An Unofficial Coloring Book for Fans of Schitt's Creek
VALENTIN RAMON